# UP YOUR NOSE

BY Seth Fishman

ILLUSTRATED BY Isabel Greenberg

Greenwillow Books
*An Imprint of HarperCollins Publishers*

For Kirby, who's been up my nose since the beginning—S. F.

Up Your Nose
Text copyright © 2022 by Seth Fishman
Illustrations copyright © 2022 by Isabel Greenberg
All rights reserved. Manufactured in Italy.
For information address HarperCollins Children's Books,
a division of HarperCollins Publishers,
195 Broadway, New York, NY 10007.
www.harpercollinschildrens.com

The full-color art was prepared digitally.
The text type is 20-point Abadi MT.

Library of Congress Cataloging-in-Publication Data

Names: Fishman, Seth, author.
Title: Up your nose / Seth Fishman ; illustrated by Isabel Greenberg.
Description: First edition. |
New York : Greenwillow Books, an Imprint of HarperCollins Publishers, 2022. |
Summary: "An exploration of the five main types of germs—
bacteria, viruses, protozoa, fungi, and helminths—
and the human immune system that protects us against them"—Provided by publisher.
Identifiers: LCCN 2021055306 | ISBN 9780062953384 (hardcover)
Subjects: LCSH: Bacteria. | Viruses. | Protozoa. | Fungi. | Helminths. | Immune system.
Classification: LCC QR75 .F54 2022 | DDC 579.3—dc23/eng/20211221
LC record available at https://lccn.loc.gov/2021055306

First Edition

22 23 24 25 26 RTLO 10 9 8 7 6 5 4 3 2 1

GREENWILLOW BOOKS

# WHY ARE THERE SO MANY RULES?

You've heard of germs, but have you *seen* them?

What we think of as germs are actually superduper tiny organisms called microbes. And they hang out *everywhere*, including on and *inside* you.

There are quadrillions of different microbes out there.

Hundreds of billions could be in the room with you right now.

But most fall into five different types:

BACTERIA

VIRUSES

# BACTERIA

Your body is made of trillions of cells, little building blocks for each part of you. Bacteria are made of only one simple cell. But that cell can come in many different shapes and (small) sizes. Some are spheres, some are spirals, and some are rods.

Bacteria can survive in all sorts of environments, from hot sulfur vents on the bottom of the ocean to glacial ice sheets. Hot, cold, and *old*—scientists have found bacteria in fossils dating back 3.5 billion years.

# VIRUSES

Viruses are smaller and simpler than bacteria, and are not even complex enough to have a cell.

A virus survives by attaching to a host's cell, taking control of it, and using the cell to make more virus. That is how they spread through your body. Ugh!

# PROTOZOA

Protozoa are made of a single cell, like bacteria. But they are bigger and have more parts, and look fun to play with. Sometimes they travel as guests of a mosquito, and often they love the water, and can be found in lakes, streams, or, of course, inside of you!

# HELMINTHS

Helminths start small like the other microbes, but they can grow up to eighty feet long! Helminths are worms with either flat or round bodies. They often live in your belly and, unlike protozoa, don't look very fun to play with.

# FUNGI

Fungi are the most complex microbe. They can be made of more than one cell, and they can appear in many forms. Like helminths, some fungi grow and grow and grow until we can see them. In fact, molds and mushrooms are both fungi! Fungi feed on plants and animals.

Now you know what germs are. You know they can be found everywhere. But do you know WHERE everywhere? Not sure you're gonna like this answer . . .

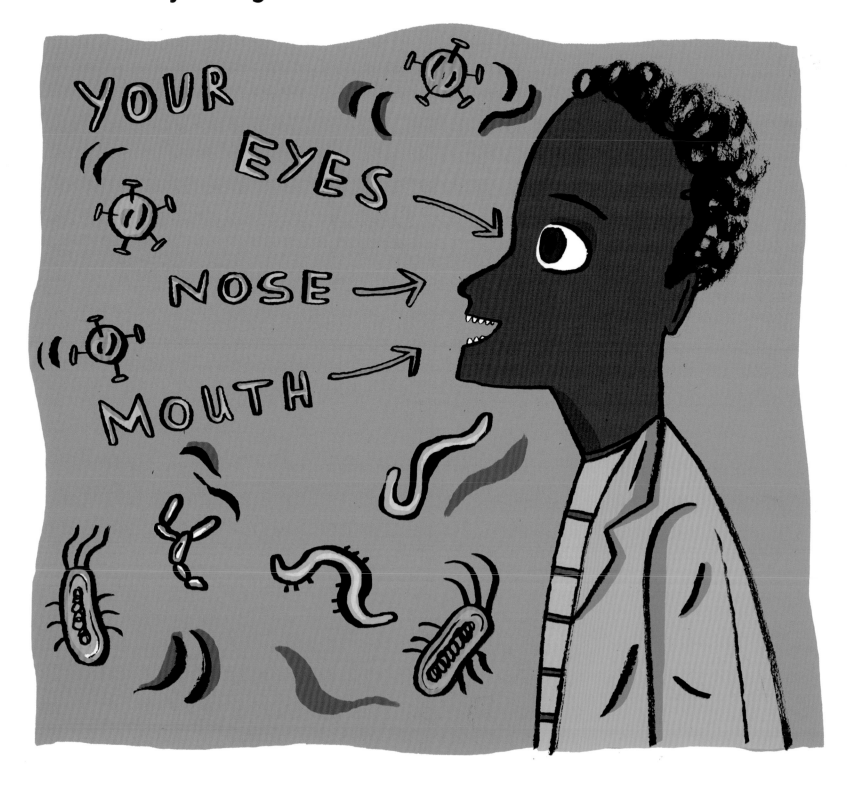

It's a lot like that song "Head, Shoulders, Knees, and Toes." In fact, if you weigh fifty pounds, you could have up to one and a half pounds of bacteria inside you right now!

Germs like to travel far beyond your body, too.
No offense, but even germs don't want to stay up your nose!

Flushing the **toilet** shoots germs six feet into the air in an invisible geyser of disgusting fun.

Careful, there are ten times more germs on your parent's **phone** than on a toilet seat!

Whether for the hot or cold water, **faucets** are a favorite vacation destination for germs!

# Let's take a tour of a germ's favorite household destinations.

ANYWHERE YOU TOUCH WITH YOUR HANDS

The easiest way to get rid of germs is to scrub those hands.

And don't just splash water on them.

You need to swirl soap all over for at least twenty seconds. That's how long it takes to say "pretty protozoa" twenty times. But what happens if you forget?

Germs might sneak inside your body in tons of different ways.

Maybe from drinking water that isn't clean, or a mosquito bite, or forgetting to wash your hands after the playground or high-fiving a friend.

Depending on the germ, you could get a sore throat, a cold, the flu, an itchy rash, or more serious illnesses. They can even make your body move, grow, or think more slowly.

But don't worry! Your amazing body has built-in defenses called the immune system to keep you safe from unwanted germs.

SKIN

TEARS

Your skin blocks most germs from getting into your body.

Tears in your eyes and the mucous linings in your nose and lungs help keep those parts safe, too.

Doctors and scientists are always discovering ways to help out the immune system. These are your body's bodyguards!

# BODYGUARD NUMBER ONE: MEDICINE

**MEDICINES** treat a sickness. That bubble gum-flavored stuff helps lower fevers and makes aches go away.

# BODYGUARD NUMBER TWO: VACCINES

VACCINES prevent sicknesses. Those small, slightly annoying shots provide your immune system with the secret plans to identify and destroy viruses and bacteria.

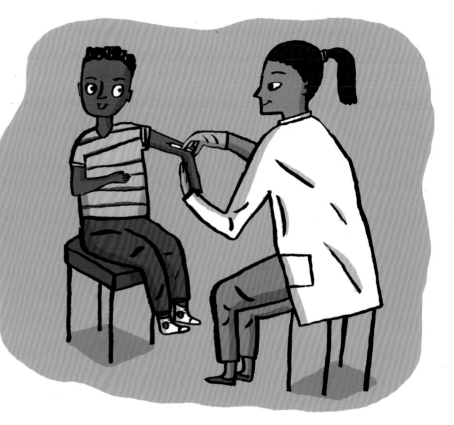

# BODYGUARD NUMBER THREE: YOU

But *you* could be the best defense of all. Help yourself by washing your hands, eating healthy, exercising, and getting plenty of sleep so your body is better prepared to fight off unwanted guests.

But wait! Not all germs are *un*wanted. In fact, some germs even *help* you live a healthy life. You have bacteria living in your intestine, for instance, that help you digest your food.

Even if you get some nasty bacteria, there are viruses that can help you fight them off.

And fungi help trees communicate and fight
illnesses, keep forests clean by breaking
down discarded foods and plants,
and even provide a tasty treat
to eat on pizzas and in salads.

Germs are part of the world, and they are a part of you. We are their entire universe.

Your nose is their living room. Your belly is their swimming pool. Your teeth are their playgrounds, and your sneezes are their rocket ships.

If you take care of yourself, you take care of the germs that are helping you, and keep those bad germs away. Protecting yourself means you protect your body and everyone around you.

So next time your parents tell you to blow your nose,

DO IT !

But also put that snot rag *gently* into the trash can. It's carrying lots of your germ buddies.

## AUTHOR'S NOTE

Even though no one likes getting sick, I hope this book has shown you that germs don't mean any harm. These simple creatures are following their own simple ways of life, trying to survive in a world filled with giant creatures called humans. (That's *you!*) And so our job is to figure out how to live *with* germs, because they certainly will be living with us.

Scientists and doctors do research to learn more about all the different types of germs and how to protect us from the harmful ones. If you think about it, every time we get sick is an opportunity to discover more about germs. Your sneezes are science experiments! What are some of the things scientists have learned?

Bacteria can release toxic (that means poisonous) materials into your body that can cause all sorts of pain and sickness. They also can group together and create a structure known as a biofilm, like the plaque on your teeth. To stop bacteria, we've developed powerful medicines known as antibiotics. They are so strong that doctors have to be careful when giving them to you, so that the antibiotics don't hurt too many of your *good* bacteria friends!

If protozoa are swimming in the water you drink, or a mosquito carrying protozoa bites you, it can cause bellyaches, diarrhea, and other infections. The best way to treat protozoa is preventative, by cleaning the water you drink. That's why you filter water when you're out in nature. Still, if you do get sick with protozoa, doctors use antiprotozoals to treat them.

Remember how fungi live in warm, damp areas? If they find those kinds of places on your body—like in between your toes—get ready for *itch city*. Antifungals are the commonly used treatment for fungi, and these usually come in the form of lotions or ointments that you rub on the itchy spots!

When a virus takes over your cells, it can cause a cold or a number of more serious illnesses. The SARS-CoV-2 virus causes COVID-19. This illness has many different symptoms, such as a sore throat, headache, tiredness, muscle aches, a bad cough, and difficulty breathing. That single virus impacted the world in some devastating ways, but scientists worked hard to make a few vaccines to protect everyone. These vaccines did an amazing job training the body to recognize COVID-19 and defend against it.

And it's not just the medicines that scientists research that help us stay safe. Your body has an incredibly complex defensive system known as the immune system. Your immune system goes into action the second you're born, acting like a shield and protecting you. Your skin, the mucus in your lungs, the liquid coating your eyes, and even the SNOT IN YOUR NOSE are part of your first line of defense. They are designed, in part, to stop germs from getting into your body.

But if any germs *do* manage to get inside, other fun-sounding body parts, such as your spleen, thyroid, lymph nodes, and even your bones are another layer of protection. They create special cells that do all sorts of amazing things. One type of white blood cell called a lymphocyte includes both B and T cells. The B cells identify and stick to intruders, blaring alarms that attract the T cells to come and hunt and destroy the invaders. Another type of white blood cell, the neutrophil, is known to attach to bacteria, and doctors actually check your blood to see if they can find neutrophils in order to confirm that you have a bacterial infection (and then treat it!).

Every day your body is fighting a battle to preserve your health, so let's make sure to give it all the help it can get! Washing your hands, eating healthy, sleeping well, and wearing a mask aren't just silly rules your parents have. They are good ways to protect yourself. Help your body help yourself, and germs will (mostly) be welcome houseguests.

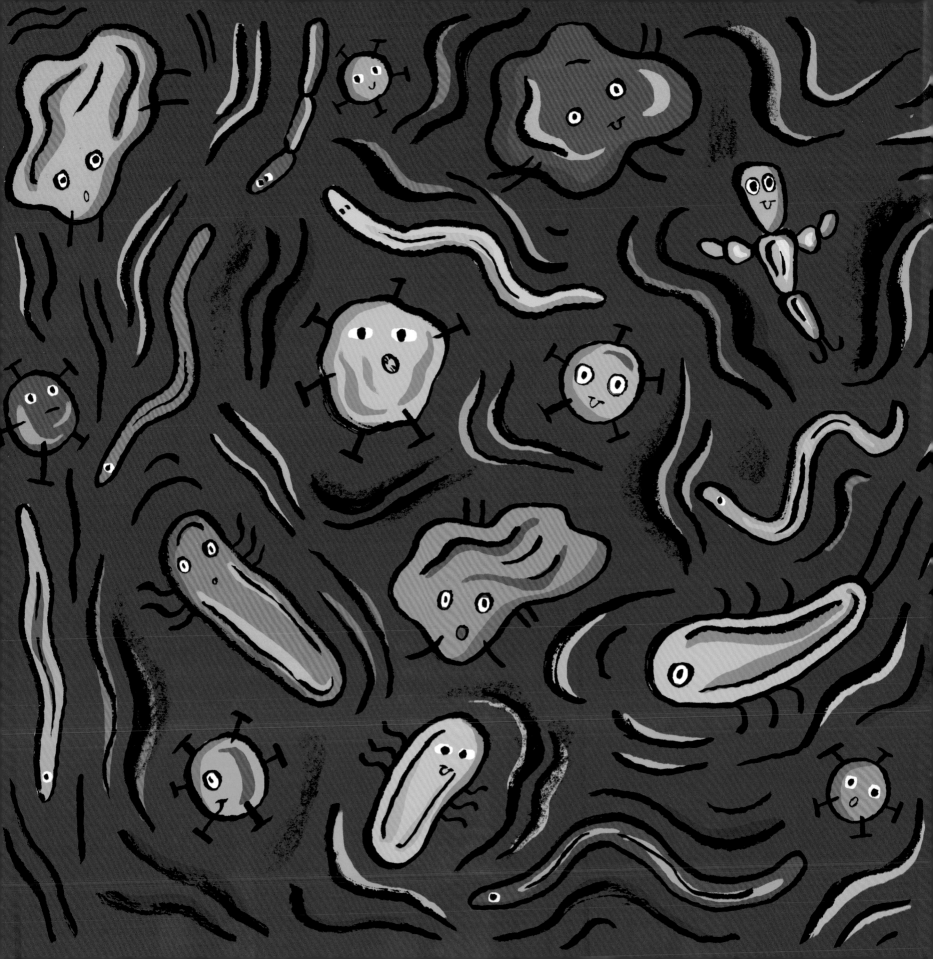